Cottage Line, Ocean Front, North of Virginia Avenue,
Virginia Beach, Va.

The cottage line and
oceanfront north of Virginia
Avenue. Circa 1908-12; $8

Enjoying a Sea Breeze on The Board Walk,
Virginia Beach, near Norfolk, Va.

Enjoying a sea breeze
on the boardwalk. Circa
1908-14; $8

A view of the wooden boardwalk. Postmarked 1911; $8

The beachfront. Seaside Park is in the background. Circa 1908-12; $8

Scene at the bath house. Circa 1908-12; $7

General view of Virginia Beach Pavilion. Handwritten message on the backside reads: "Am on the sand hills chasing fiddlers today." Postmarked 1913; $8

The Infant Sanitarium. Circa 1908-12; $10

The Arlington Hotel. Printed message on the backside reads: "Situated directly facing the shore, giving easy access to the beach, and board walk, very popular affording good accommodations to visitors and patrons." Circa 1907-12; $10

First Baptist Church,
Va. Beach, Va.

The First Baptist Church. Postmarked 1913; $12

BOARD WALK AND BEACH AT OCEAN CASINO, VIRGINIA BEACH, VA.

122701

Boardwalk and beach at the Ocean Casino. Circa 1920s; $7

The Martha Washington Hotel and Apartments. Printed message on the backside reads: "Five blocks south from New Ocean Casino. Three new modern brick buildings, overlooking the ocean from the East and Lake Holly from the West. So situated that no matter from which direction the wind blows every guest room has wafted to it the sweetness of the health-giving sea breezes. 122 rooms and furnished apartments, 105 with baths. Every room outside, telephone, lights, closets, hot and cold water, clean beds of tempting softness. Meals of superior quality served all day for your convenience." The hotel was located at Atlantic Avenue and 8th Street. Circa 1920s; $7

MARTHA WASHINGTON HOTEL AND APARTMENTS, VIRGINIA BEACH, VA.

OCEAN AND LAKE FRONTAGE

COOLEST LOCATION.

J. WESLEY GARDNER, MANAGING OWNER, ATLANTIC AVE. & 8TH ST.

113174

A VIEW OF THE BEACH, VIRGINIA BEACH, VA.

A view of the beach. Circa 1920s; $6

NEW PAVILION, VIRGINIA BEACH, VA.

The New Pavilion. Circa 1916-25; $8

Night view of gardens and Cavalier Hotel. Printed message on the backside reads: "New community hotel erected by popular stock subscriptions. Occupying a 60 acre tract which includes an 18 hole golf course. The architecture and landscaping typify the traditional colonial plantation atmosphere of Virginia. Here the salt tang of the sea is mingled with the aromatic redolence of pines." Circa 1920; $6

The Cavalier Hotel. Circa 1920s; $6

The Cavalier Hotel and gardens at night. Circa 1920s; $6

Night view of the Cavalier Hotel. Handwritten message on the backside reads: "Water fine, weather hot. Wish you had a vacation to come down here." Circa 1920s; $6

116365

The swimming pool of the Cavalier Hotel. Handwritten message on the backside reads: "This is a beautiful hotel and it only cost $14.00 per day to stop there. You can look at the ocean all day from the hotel. Everyone around here almost lives at the beach in the summer months." Circa 1920s; $7

OCEAN FRONT, SHOWING TAIT COTTAGE, VIRGINIA BEACH, VA.

Oceanfront showing the Tait Cottage. In the 1920s this cottage was enlarged and renamed the Princess Anne Hotel. Circa 1920s; $10

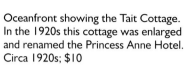

PRINCESS ANNE HOTEL, VIRGINIA BEACH, VIRGINIA.

The Princess Anne Hotel. This was the second hotel at Virginia Beach to be so named. The first Princess Anne Hotel burned in 1907. Postmarked 1925; $8

The Princess Anne Hotel on the Ocean. Printed message on the backside reads: "One of the most popular hotels of the beautiful resort with 110 thoroughly modern rooms facing the ocean." Circa 1920s; $8

PRINCESS ANNE HOTEL ON THE OCEAN, VIRGINIA BEACH, VA.

113601

LIVING ROOM, PRINCESS ANNE HOTEL, VIRGINIA BEACH, VA.

The living room of the Princess Anne Hotel. Circa 1920s; $8

PICNIC PAVILION AND NEW OCEAN CASINO. VIRGINIA BEACH. VA.

Picnic Pavilion and new Ocean Casino. Circa 1920s; $10

THE WALK ALONG THE SHORE. VIRGINIA BEACH. VA.

The walk along the shore. Circa 1920s; $6

ON THE SANDS AT VIRGINIA BEACH. FAMOUS SEASHORE RESORT. NEAR NORFOLK. V

4133-29

On the sands at Virginia Beach. Circa 1920s; $6

TRAYMORE APARTMENTS AND PINEWOOD HOTEL, VIRGINIA BEACH, VA.

Traymore Apartments and the Pinewood Hotel. Circa 1920s; $7

VIEW OF BEACH AFTER A STORM, LOOKING NORTH FROM NEAR 17TH STREET, VIRGINIA BEACH, VA.

View of the beach after a storm looking north from near 17th Street. Circa 1920s; $7

PRINCESS ANNE COUNTRY CLUB, VIRGINIA BEACH, VA.

Princess Anne Country Club. Circa 1920s; $7

OCEAN FRONT AND COTTAGE LINE, VIRGINIA BEACH, VA.

The oceanfront and cottage line.
Circa 1920s; $8

The Courtney Terrace Hotel.
Printed message on the backside
reads: "One of the newer beach
front hotels. Accommodations
unexcelled directly on the boardwalk facing the Atlantic Ocean."
Circa 1920s; $7

COURTNEY TERRACE, VIRGINIA BEACH, NEAR NORFOLK, VA

106460

PINEWOOD HOTEL AND APARTMENTS, VIRGINIA BEACH, VA.

Pinewood Hotel and Apartments.
Circa 1920s; $7

CHALFONTE HOTEL, VIRGINIA BEACH, VA.

The Chalfonte Hotel.
Circa 1920s; $10

25

BEACH FRONT AND COTTAGES FROM NEW OCEAN CASINO LOOKING NORTH, VIRGINIA BEACH, VA.

113168

Beach front and cottages from new Ocean Casino looking north. Circa 1920s; $8

GOLF LINKS, PRINCESS ANNE COUNTRY CLUB, VIRGINIA BEACH, VA.

86070

Golf links, Princess Anne Country Club. Circa 1920s; $7

NEW CASINO, VIRGINIA BEACH, VA.

New Casino. Postmarked 1920; $8

THE POOL SEASIDE PARK, VIRGINIA BEACH, VA

The pool at Seaside Park. Circa 1920s; $8

122699

SEASIDE PARK AND BEACH, VIRGINIA BEACH, VA

Seaside Park and beach. Circa 1920s; $8

ENTRANCE TO BEACH FROM BATH HOUSES, NEW SECTION, VIRGINIA BEACH, VA.

Entrance to the beach from the bath houses. Circa 1920s; $7

CLUB HOUSE, PRINCESS ANNE COUNTRY CLUB, VIRGINIA BEACH, VA.

Copyright by H. C. Mann.

Club House, Princess
Anne Country Club.
Circa 1920s; $8

NEW PAVILION AND BASEMENT BATH HOUSE, VIRGINIA BEACH, VA.

New pavilion and basement bath house. Circa 1920s; $8

NEW OCEAN CASINO AND COTTAGE LINE, LOOKING SOUTH, VIRGINIA BEACH, VA.

113161

New Ocean Casino and cottage line, looking south. Handwritten message on the backside reads: "We would have lots of fun if it just wouldn't rain so much." Postmarked 1925; $7

PRINCESS ANNE HOTEL ON THE ATLANTIC OCEAN, VIRGINIA BEACH, VA.

Princess Anne Hotel on the Atlantic Ocean. Circa 1920s; $8

PRINCESS ANNE HOTEL, VIRGINIA BEACH, VA.

The Princess Anne Hotel. Circa 1920s; $8

CASINO FROM ENTRANCE, VIRGINIA BEACH, VA.

Casino from entrance. Handwritten message on the backside reads: "Sister Anne and I are enjoying the ocean breeze immensely." Postmarked 1923; $8

GALILEON CHAPEL AND COTTAGES, OCEAN FRONT, VIRGINIA BEACH, VA.

Galileon Chapel and cottages, ocean front. Postmarked 1924; $7

General View of Virginia Beach, Va.

General view of Virginia Beach. Circa 1920s; $8

Newcastle Hotel. Circa 1920s; $7

Flower beds and cottage line. Circa 1920s; $6

The Waverley Hotel. Circa 1920s; $6

The bathing beach.
Circa 1920s; $6

SEASIDE PARK ON THE ATLANTIC, VIRGINIA BEACH, VA.

OPEN AIR SALT WATER SWIMMING POOLS AT VIRGINIA BEACH, VA. NEAR NORFOLK, VA.

VIRGINIA BEACH, VA.

Two views of Seaside Park. At first the postcards look the same, but a close look reveals that they are very different from each other. Circa 1920s; $8

Bathers at Virginia Beach. Circa 1920s; $6

Scene at entrance to casino grounds. Circa 1920s; $8

Scene at Entrance to Casino Grounds, Virginia Beach, Va.

33

PRINCESS ANNE COUNTRY CLUB, VIRGINIA BEACH, NEAR NORFOLK, VA.—38

15th Green

PHOTO COURTESY. NORFOLK PORTSMOUTH CH

The Princess Anne Country Club. Printed message on the backside reads: "Regardless of the number of times a golfer plays Princess Anne, its charms are so varied as to be even more attractive for the next day of play. Situated as it is on the Atlantic Ocean and cut through a virgin forest of tall pine trees, it is ideal. Its eighteen holes test and discipline the golfer in the earliest days of his game and thrill and defy him when he thinks his game is perfect." Postmarked 1938; $7

Coast Guard Station from the boardwalk. Circa 1930s; $6

COAST GUARD STATION. VIRGINIA BEACH. VA.

38540

COURTNEY TERRACE, VIRGINIA BEACH, NEAR NORFOLK, VA.

4A-H1631

The Courtney Terrace Hotel. Circa 1930s; $7

GENERAL OCEAN FRONT VIEW, VIRGINIA BEACH, VA.

General view of the cottage line from the ocean. Circa 1930s; $6

GREETINGS from VIRGINIA BEACH VA.

80

Large letter greetings from Virginia Beach. Circa 1930s; $6

35

PRINCESS ANNE COUNTRY CLUB HOUSE. VIRGINIA BEACH. VA.

61695

The Princess Anne Country Club House. Circa 1930s; $7

83:-FIGUREHEAD, VIRGINIA BEACH, VA.

47541

The figurehead of the wrecked vessel, the *Dictator*, looks out to sea. Circa 1930s; $6

SEASIDE PARK, VIRGINIA BEACH, VA.   57

64483

Air view of Seaside Park. Circa 1930s; $7

Cavalier Hotel Beach Club, Virginia Beach, Va.

Cavalier Hotel Beach Club. Circa 1920s; $6

NEW WAVERLY HOTEL AND BEACH PLAZA, VIRGI...

New Waverly Hotel and beach plaza.
Circa 1930s; $6

47662

The Virginia Lee Hotel. Circa 1930s; $7

39

The Courtney Terrace Hotel. The hotel was located at 16th Street and oceanfront. Circa 1930s; $7

Music room and foyer of the Albemarle Hall. Printed message on the backside reads: "Albemarle Hall has been remodeled and every modern convenience has been provided for the comfort of guests. Facing the ocean are spacious verandas where lovers of the sea may sit for hours drinking in the expanse of beauty reaching to the horizon." Circa 1930s; $6

Interior view of the Excellent Restaurant. The restaurant was located on Atlantic Avenue between 16th and 17th Streets. It was open twenty-four hours a day and specialized in fried chicken, seafood, and Italian spaghetti. Circa 1930s; $7

The oceanfront hotels. Circa 1930s; $6

38-:THE CAVALIER FROM SUNKEN GARDEN, VIRGINIA BEACH, VA.

The Cavalier from sunken gardens. Handwritten message on the backside reads: "The boat ride was wonderful. I was out on the beach awhile today. I don't wanta come home."
Circa 1930s; $6

THE CAVALIER HOTEL AND BEACH CLUB, VIRGINIA BEACH VIRGINIA

The Cavalier Hotel and Beach Club. Circa 1930s; $7

41

P I N E W O O D   H O T E L
VIRGINIA BEACH, VIRGINIA

5A-H1481

The Pinewood Hotel. Printed message on the backside reads: "Located on 225 feet of ocean frontage. Open all year, fireproof, all outside rooms each with private or connecting bath." Circa 1930s; $7

BEACH PLAZA HOTEL, VIRGINIA BEACH, VIRGINIA

The Beach Plaza Hotel. Circa 1930s; $7

THE PINEWOOD HOTEL

VIRGINIA BEACH, VIRGINIA

The Pinewood Hotel. Printed message on the backside reads: "Sports on our own grounds – handball, badminton, tennis, shuffleboard, etc." Postmarked 1938; $7

43

88:-AERIAL VIEW SHOWING CAVALIER HOTEL BEACH CLUB.

PRINCESS ANNE GOLF CLUB, AND COTTAGES, VIRGINIA BEACH, VA.   47546

Air view showing the Cavalier Hotel Beach Club. Circa 1930s; $6

The Cavalier Hotel. Printed message on the backside reads: "The aristocrat of Virginia's seashore." Circa 1930s; $6

Air view of the Cavalier Hotel. Circa 1930s; $6

SPOTSWOOD ARMS — VIRGINIA BEACH, VA.

Directly on the Ocean Front and Ocean Promenade   D-5163

The Spotswood Arms. Printed message on the backside reads: "Ocean front at 26th Street. Conveniently located in the center of all beach activities. It is the ideal resort home. Unsurpassed 'Old Virginia Cooked Meals.' All bedrooms attractively and comfortably furnished." Circa 1930s; $7

44

TRAYMORE HOTEL — OCEAN FRONT AT NINTH STREET — VIRGINIA BEACH, VIRGINIA

The Traymore Hotel, oceanfront at Ninth Street. Circa 1930s; $6

BEACH SCENE SOUTH OF COAST GUARD STATION BY NIGHT, VIRGINIA BEACH, VA.

Beach scene south of Coast Guard Station by night.
Circa 1930s; $6

Hotel Warner, Virginia Beach, Va.

The Hotel Warner. Printed message on the backside reads: "Hotel Warner, newest and finest on the ocean front, located at 34th Street." Circa 1930s; $7

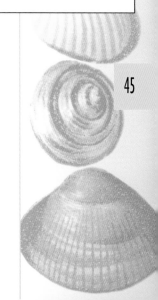

45

NEW WAVERLEY HOTEL, VIRGINIA BEACH, VA.

The New Waverley Hotel. Circa 1930s; $6

U. S. COAST GUARD STATION, VIRGINIA BEACH, VA.

4A-H1638

The U.S. Coast Guard Station. Circa 1930s; $7

The Princess Anne Golf Club. Circa 1930s; $6

The Cavalier Country Club. Circa 1930s; $6

The Cavalier Beach Club. Circa 1930s; $6

The Gay Manor Hotel. Printed message on the backside reads: "Virginia Beach's newest and most modern hotel. Ocean front at 39th Street." Circa 1930s; $7

The Cavalier Beach Club. Postmarked 1935; $10

The Cavalier Beach Club. Circa 1930s; $10

The Cavalier Hotel. Circa 1930s; $10

The Cavalier Hotel. Postmarked 1937; $10

The Terrace Slope at the Cavalier Hotel. Circa 1930s; $10

The Sunken Garden at the Cavalier Hotel. Circa 1930s; $10

The Cavalier Hotel. Circa 1930s; $10

The Cavalier Hotel. Circa 1930s; $10

The bathing beach. Circa 1930s; $12

The Idlewhyle Hotel. Circa 1930s; $7

PARAMOUNT
The Superb Air Conditioned Restaurant of Virginia Beach, Va.

BEAUTIFUL BALCONY FOR BANQUETS

The Paramount Restaurant. The restaurant was located at the corner of 18th Street and Atlantic Avenue. Printed message on the backside reads: "Catering to the most discriminate. Fine well prepared foods by Virginia's foremost chefs. Our steaks, chops, and seafood specialties are a remembrance. Managed and personally supervised by its owner, you may be assured that your meals, and banquets too, will be enjoyed here, in splendid atmosphere." Circa 1930s; $8

TRAFTON INN, OCEAN AVE., BETWEEN 23RD AND 24TH STREET, VIRGINIA BEACH, VA.

The Trafton Inn, Ocean Avenue, between 23rd and 24th Street. Postmarked 1938; $7

41854

The Brockmyer, 206 20th St., Virginia Beach, Virginia.

The Brockmyer at 20th Street. Circa 1930s; $7

Busy Atlantic Avenue. Handwritten
message on the backside reads:
"We have had great weather and
enjoyed it all. Will be home soon."
Circa 1930s; $8

Atlantic Avenue, Virginia Beach, Va.

Air Conditioned　　Normandie Restaurant, Virginia Beach, Va.

80042

Interior view of the Normandie Restaurant. The restaurant was located at 2112 Atlantic Avenue. Circa 1930s; $7

OCEAN PROMENADE, VIRGINIA BEACH, NEAR NORFOLK, VA.—28

The ocean promenade.
Circa 1930s; $6

VIRGINIA BEACH, NEAR NORFOLK, VA.—29

Enjoying the beach
and ocean surf.
Circa 1930s; $6

Daniel Boone Monument, Virginia Beach, Va.   V-30

64488

The Daniel Boone Marker. Printed message on the backside reads: "Monument marking end of Daniel Boone Trail at Virginia Beach. The marker stands on the brink of the Atlantic Ocean at Seventeenth Street, Virginia Beach, where it is claimed Boone stood when he first beheld the rolling waters of the Atlantic Ocean." Circa 1940s; $6

Air View of Surf Club, Virginia Beach, Va.   V-32

64485

Air view of Surf Club. Circa 1940s; $7

PRINCESS ANNE HOTEL
Virginia Beach, Va.
Ocean Front Dining Room

The Princess Anne Hotel. Printed message on the backside reads: "One of the most popular hotels of this beautiful resort with 110 thoroughly modern rooms facing the Atlantic Ocean." Circa 1940s; $7

Fair Sun Worshippers at the Cavalier Beach Club, Virginia Beach, Va.

Fair sun worshippers at the Cavalier Beach Club. Circa 1940s; $10

BICYCLE RIDING ALONG THE WALK, VIRGINIA BEACH, VA.

49905

Bicycle riding along the walk. Circa 1940s; $6

56

Princess Anne Country Club House. Virginia Beach, Va. 38

The Princess Anne Country Club House. Circa 1940s; $6

U.S. Coast Guard Station. Circa 1940s; $6

General view of Virginia Beach. One of America's popular shore resorts. Circa 1940s; $6

The boardwalk, looking south. Circa 1940s; $6

Atlantic Avenue looking north. Circa 1940s; $6

17th Street from Atlantic Avenue. Circa 1940s; $7

View from the Cavalier Hotel, showing tennis court, pony track, and beach club. Circa 1940s; $6

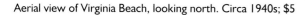

Surf Bathing, Virginia Beach, Va.

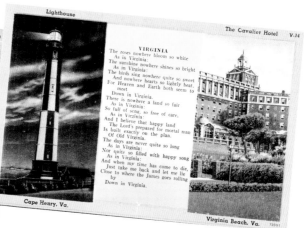

Lighthouse

The Cavalier Hotel V-14

VIRGINIA

The roses nowhere bloom so white
As in Virginia.
The sunshine nowhere shines so bright
As in Virginia:
The birds sing nowhere quite so sweet,
And nowhere hearts so lightly beat,
For Heaven and Earth both seem to
meet
Down in Virginia.
There is nowhere a land so fair
As in Virginia.
So full of song, so free of care,
As in Virginia:
And I believe that happy land
The Lord's prepared for mortal man
Is built exactly on the plan,
Of Old Virginia.
The days are never quite so long
As in Virginia:
Nor quite so filled with happy song
As in Virginia:
And when my time has come to die,
Just take me back and let me lie
Close to where the James goes rolling
by
Down in Virginia.

Cape Henry, Va.

Virginia Beach, Va.

Aerial view of Virginia Beach, looking north. Circa 1940s; $5

Surf bathing at Virginia Beach. Circa 1940s; $5

The lighthouse at Cape Henry and the Cavalier Hotel. Circa 1940s; $5

8—Looking North from 22nd Street, Virginia Beach, Va.

8A-H3088

Looking north from 22nd Street. Circa 1940s; $5

59

The Martha Washington Hotel and Apartments at oceanfront and 8th Street. Circa 1940s; $6

Another view of the Martha Washington Hotel and Apartments. Circa 1940s; $6

49846

The Burtonia. Printed message on the backside reads: "The Burtonia – in the heart of Virginia Beach. One block from the ocean. Near new 900 foot fishing pier. We quote the following rates: June 15 to Labor Day – Single per week $21.00, double per week $25.00." Circa 1940s; $6

3—Beach and Cottage Line Looking South, Virginia Beach, Va.

9A-H2144

The beach and cottage line looking south. Circa 1940s; $5

MARTY'S LOBSTER HOUSE
33rd and Atlantic Ave.
Virginia Beach, Va.
Ph. GARDEN 8-5681

Marty's Lobster House, 33rd and Atlantic Avenue. Printed message on the backside reads: "Virginia Beach's famous seafood restaurant. Specializing in Maine lobster – Kansas City steaks – chicken." Circa 1940s; $7

ALBEMARLE HALL. ENTRANCE FROM ATLANTIC BOULEVARD. VIRGINIA BEACH, VA.

Albemarle Hall, entrance from Atlantic Boulevard. Circa 1940s; $7

The figurehead from the ship *Dictator* that wrecked off shore from 40th street in 1891. Circa 1940s; $6

The Waverly Hotel on the ocean at 22nd Street. Circa 1940s; $6

The boardwalk. Circa 1940s; $6

The Coast Guard Station. Circa 1940s; $8

The Coral Sand. Printed message on the backside reads: "Guest house – 23rd Street. Located in the center of activities, 1/2 block from ocean. Excellent accommodations." Circa 1940s; $7

The United States Post Office. Circa 1940s; $6

Water skiing at yacht and country club. Circa 1940s; $6

Printed message on the backside reads: "Scene at tea dance at Cavalier Hotel Beach Club." Circa 1940s; $6

Printed message on the backside reads: "Finest private beach on the east coast in front of Cavalier Hotel Beach Club." Circa 1940s; $6

GAY MANOR HOTEL, VIRGINIA BEACH, VA.

46992

The Gay Manor Hotel. Circa 1940s; $6

72065

Cabanas along the boardwalk. Circa 1940s; $6

Terrace Beach Club, Virginia Beach, Va.

9A-H1514

The Terrace Beach Club.
Circa 1940s; $6

The bathing beach from the
boardwalk. Circa 1940s; $5

86:-BATHING BEACH, VIRGINIA BEACH, VA.

47366

The Princess Anne Hotel. Printed message on the backside reads: "The Princess Anne Hotel has just undergone a new remodeling program and has added a number of new modernistic ocean front rooms to its properties. We excel in fine southern cooking." Circa 1940s; $5

Aerial view of Virginia Beach. Circa 1950s; $5

Bird's-eye view of boardwalk and beach. Circa 1950s; $5

Mayflower Apartments, Virginia Beach, Va.

83141

The Mayflower Apartments. The sixteen story building was completed in 1951 and stands at 34th Street and Atlantic Avenue. Circa 1951; $5

Beautiful Virginia Beach, Virginia Beach, Virginia

5C-H541

Busy beach from the boardwalk. Circa 1950s; $5

Aerial View of Virginia Beach, Virginia

5C-H536

Aerial view of Virginia Beach. Circa 1950s; $5

Manson's Motel at 2800 to 2804 Pacific Avenue. Printed message on the backside reads: "30 rooms with private and semi-private baths, all rooms opening to screened porches." Circa 1950s; $5

The Greenwood Hotel. Street. Printed message on the backside reads: "On the ocean at 20th Street. Circulating hot water, private and semi-private baths, also heated rooms. Located in the heart of the beach. Look for the green dorman (sic) sign." Circa 1950s; $6

On the beach at the Sea Horse. Handwritten message on the backside reads: "This probably looks familiar to you. We have a very nice lifeguard named Audy." Postmarked 1953; $6

ON THE BEACH AT THE SEA HORSE, VIRGINIA BEACH, VA.

The Cavalier Beach and Cabana Club. Handwritten message on the backside reads: "We are having a very nice time here. We're getting such nice tans." Circa 1950s; $5

VIRGINIA BEACH, VIRGINIA

The boardwalk. Handwritten message on the backside reads: "Hi vacationers from fellow vacationers." Postmarked 1957; $5

Neptune's Corner Restaurant at 31st and Atlantic Avenue. Printed message on the backside reads: "Famous for seashore dinners, whole broiled flounders, steaks, chops, and chicken. Our food has been carefully purchased and cooked in a fashion you and your family will enjoy." Postmarked 1959; $6

The Gulf Stream Hotel at Atlantic Avenue and 29th Street. Printed message on the backside reads: "Virginia Beach's finest moderate priced hotel. Overlooking the ocean in the center of resort life. All rooms with outside view and private bath. Summer rates $4.00, $5.00, and $6.00 per person per day. Reduced rates spring and fall." Postmarked 1954; $6

The Homestead by the Sea on the oceanfront at 23rd Street. Printed message on the backside reads: "American or European plan. Comfortable rooms with bath. Free adjacent parking." Circa 1950s; $5

The Halifax Hotel at 26th Street and Ocean Avenue. Circa 1950s; $5

The Ivanhoe at 21st Street and Atlantic Avenue. Printed message on the backside reads: Summer rates (include breakfast and dinner) Daily: $7.00 to $11.00 per person, Weekly: $42.00 to $65.00 per person. All rooms with bath. Telephone in every room. Special rates for groups of 3 or more persons in one room." Postmarked 1951; $6

The Cavalier Beach and Cabana Club. Postmarked 1952; $5

Printed message on the backside reads: "looking north from the top of the new 16 story Mayflower Apartments." Circa 1950s; $5

The Halifax Hotel at 26th Street. Postmarked 1959; $5

The Avalon Hotel at 20th Street and oceanfront. Handwritten message on the backside reads: "Our room is below the arrow." Circa 1950s; $6

The Atlantic Hotel on the oceanfront at 22nd Street. Circa 1950s; $5

The Greenwood Motor Hotel on the ocean at 20th Street. Printed message on the backside reads: "European plan. Circulating hot water, private and semi private baths, also heated rooms. Rates from $5.00 to $14.00 double. Located in the heart of the beach. Look for the green dorman (sic) sign." Circa 1950s; $5

"Virginia Beach, Virginia"

Views of Virginia Beach. Circa 1950s; $5

The Cavalier Yacht and Country Club on Link-Horn Bay. Circa 1950s; $5

The Cavalier Beach and Cabana Club. Circa 1950s; $5

Hotel Prince Charles at the ocean-front and 17th Street. Printed message on the backside reads: "All rooms with private bath. Simmons steel furniture and beautiful mattresses in every room. Radiant heating for year-round operation." Circa 1950s; $5

Looking towards the beach from the end of the 912 foot fishing pier. Circa 1960s; $5

Printed message on the backside reads: "Fishing from the 912 foot pier at Virginia Beach, located at 15th Street and Atlantic Avenue. Perch, roundheads, blue fish, sea bass, flounder, croakers, and other fish are caught here." Circa 1960s; $5

The Norwegian Lady statue, a gift of the people of Moss, Norway, in remembrance of the Norwegian ship, the *Dictator* that wrecked near 40th Street in 1891. Circa 1960s; $5

The Princess Anne Inn at 25th Street and Atlantic Avenue. Circa 1960s; $5

The Puritan Restaurant at 17th Street and Atlantic Avenue. Circa 1960s; $6

The Seahawk Motel at 26th Street and the oceanfront. Circa 1960s; $5

The Ocean Pier. Circa 1960s; $5

The Bel Harbour Motel at 13th Street and the oceanfront. Circa 1960s; $5

The Gulf Stream at Atlantic Avenue and 29th Street. Printed message on the backside reads: "A fine moderate priced family-type hotel. Nice, clean, quiet, informal. Located in the heart of the beach, overlooking the ocean. Swimming directly from room to beach." Circa 1960s; $5

Forbes Salt Water Taffy store. Circa 1960s; $5

The Thunderbird Motor Lodge at oceanfront and 35th Street. Circa 1960s; $5

The dining room at the Thunderbird Motor Lodge. Circa 1960s; $5

The Suntide Motel at oceanside and 67th Street. Circa 1960s; $5

The Bel Harbour Motel at oceanfront and 13th Street. Circa 1960s; $5

The Thunderbird Motor Lodge at
35th Street and the oceanfront.
Circa 1960s; $5

The Traymore Sea Colony at
oceanfront and 9th Street.
Circa 1960s; $5

The Virginia Beach Civic Center. Printed message on the backside reads: "This geodesic domed auditorium has 15,000 square feet of exhibit, seating and banquet space and is the ultimate in functional design." Circa 1960s; $5

Greetings from Virginia Beach. Circa 1960s; $5

The view looking north from the roof of the Mayflower Apartments. Circa 1960s; $5

89

Virginia Beach, Virginia

A summer day on the beach.
Circa 1960s; $5

The beachfront and the
Mayflower Apartments.
Circa 1960s; $5

The Ocean Reef Restaurant
at 2604 Atlantic Avenue.
Circa 1960s; $5

The boardwalk train.
Circa 1960s; $5

Handwritten message on the backside reads: "I'm down here with a friend for a few days to relax. The water is great, the sun is hot, and my sunburn hurts." Postmarked 1967; $5

Umbrellas lined up in the summer sun at Virginia Beach. Circa 1960s; $5

Beach scene at Virginia Beach. Circa 1960s; $5

The Golf Ranch Motel at 31st Street. Circa 1960s; $5

94

The Holiday Sands at oceanfront and 11th Street. Postmarked 1960; $5

The Sir Walter by the Sea at oceanfront and 39th Street. Printed message on the backside reads: "A hotel in the Virginia tradition reflecting the graciousness and charm of yesterday blended with the modern conveniences of today and tomorrow." Circa 1960s; $5

The Lighthouse Restaurant at oceanfront and Rudee Inlet. Circa 1960s; $5

The Seahawk Motel at 26th Street and oceanfront. Circa 1960s; $5

The Bel Harbour Motel at oceanfront and 13th Street. Circa 1960s; $5

The Princess Anne Inn at 25th Street and Atlantic Avenue. Circa 1960s; $6

The Ocean Ranch Motel at 32nd Street and oceanfront. Postmarked 1961; $5

The Viking Motel on Atlantic Avenue. Circa 1960s; $5

97

The Saxony Motel near 22nd Street and oceanfront. Circa 1960s; $5

The Gay Vacationer Motel at 34th Street and oceanfront. Circa 1960s; $5

The Marshalls at 66th Street and oceanfront. Circa 1960s; $5

The Marshalls on the ocean at 66th Street. Circa 1960s; $5

The Holiday Sands Motel at 11th Street and oceanfront. Circa 1960s; $5

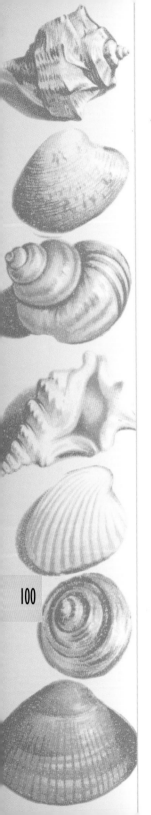

The Breakers
Motor Hotel
at 25th Street
and oceanfront.
Circa 1960s; $5

The Beach Car-
ousel Motel on
Pacific Avenue.
Circa 1960s; $5

you haven't Lived if you haven't been to ?

Virginia Beach, Va.

Virginia Beach is located on the Atlantic Ocean and is Virginia's premier bathing resort. Circa 1960s; $5

The Virginia Beach of Today

Watching the sunrise over
the Atlantic Ocean.

Watching the early morning waves.

The sun rises over the fishing pier.

Looking south from the fishing pier.

The busy beach at midday.

Sunny day at Virginia Beach.

Along the boardwalk.

Watching the waves and enjoying the sun.

The boardwalk at 20th Street.

Beachwear window display.

Virginia Beach saltwater taffy on display.

Virginia Beach volleyballs.

Along the sidewalk on Atlantic Avenue.

Storefront on Atlantic Avenue.

The Haunted Fun House on Atlantic Avenue.

Oh Fudge storefront on Atlantic Avenue.

During the summer months Atlantic Avenue is Beach Street USA.

Lifeguard watching bathers.

Looking north along the beach.

A part of the Virginia Beach skyline.

Virginia Beach skyline and hotels.

109

Looking north from the fishing pier.

Having fun on the beach and in the surf.

Summertime beach fun.

Rental bikes.

The old Coast Guard Station.

The Norwegian Lady Statue.

On the porch of the Coast Guard Station.

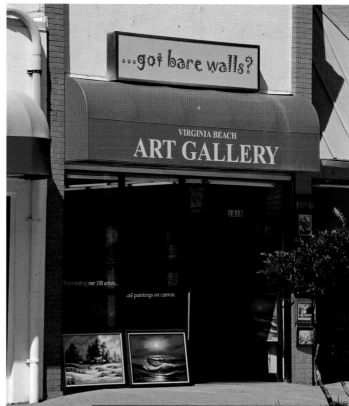

Storefront on Atlantic Avenue.

Store display on Atlantic Avenue.

The Virginia Beach skyline looking north from the fishing pier.

Looking towards shore on a summer day.

Along the oceanfront.

High rise hotels and the beach.

Storefront in the morning light along Atlantic Avenue.

A beachwear store on Atlantic Avenue.

Postcard display rack.

114

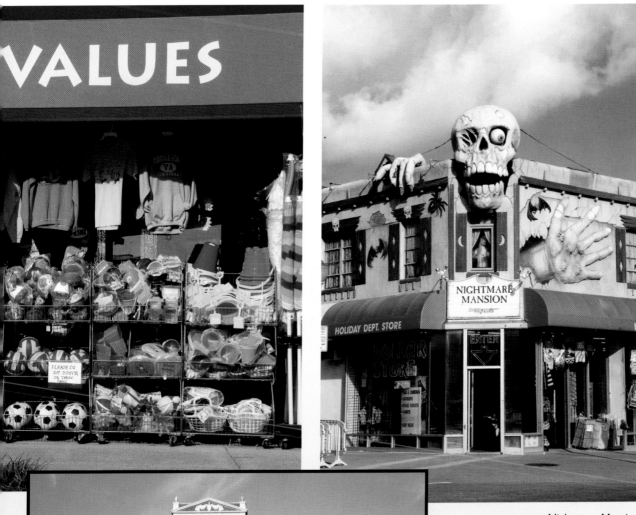

Nightmare Mansion.

The Cavalier Hotel.

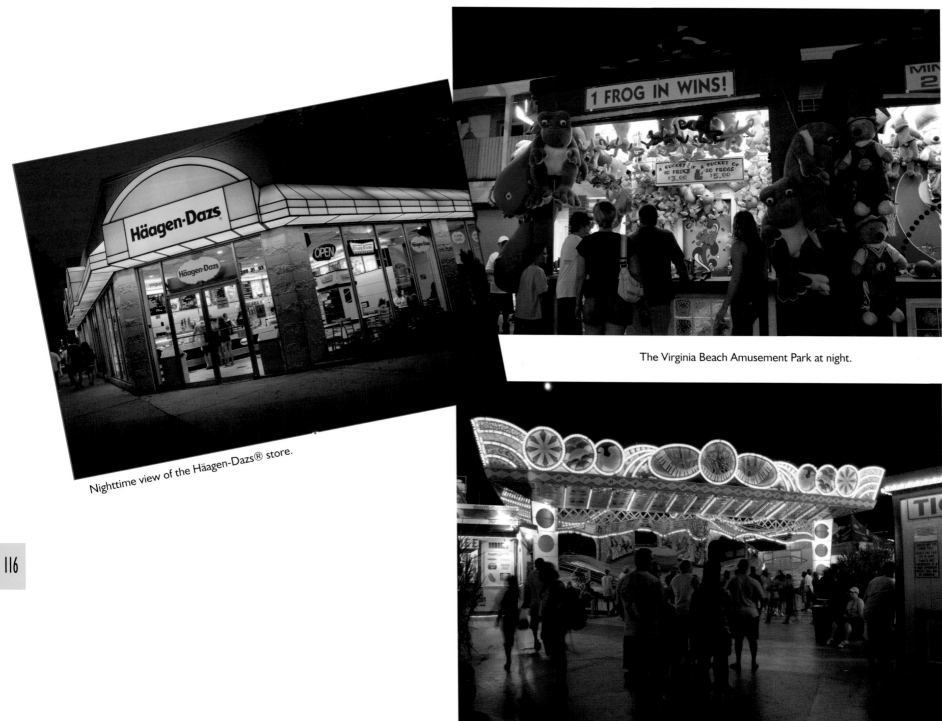

The Virginia Beach Amusement Park at night.

Nighttime view of the Häagen-Dazs® store.

The Pier Gift Shop.

Nighttime view looking towards the boardwalk.

Store window of the Candy Kitchen at night.

Dusk on Atlantic Avenue.

Bargain Beachwear storefront at night.

119

Storefront on Atlantic Avenue.

Along Atlantic Avenue at dusk.

Envy Bar & Grill on Atlantic Avenue.

A cool and clear summer night on Atlantic Avenue.

Shop on the fishing pier.

Inside Kohr Bros.

Atlantic Avenue neon.

Inside the Candy Kitchen.

Along Atlantic Avenue on a summer night.

Atlantic Avenue.

A summer night at Virginia Beach.

Dairy Queen on a busy Friday night.

Along Atlantic Avenue at night.

Nighttime view of Atlantic Avenue.